Productive PathFinder

Designing Careers That Compound:
From Potential to Purpose

By **Nigel Pinto**

The **Productive PathFinder framework** and **PathFinder Cycle**
are original concepts developed by the author.

ISBN: 979-8-9953224-0-5
Cover design: Nigel Pinto
Editing: Rachel Pinto

Published by Productive PathFinder
First Edition

Printed in the United States of America

For those who refused to let others own their path.

CONTENTS

INTRODUCTION
Seeds, Ecosystems, and the Path Forward

Careers stall because people wait

This book begins with a simple truth: no one hands you a career. You build it—slowly, intentionally, with a mindset that compounds over seasons.

Careers rarely stall because of a lack of talent. They stall when people defer action because they wait for promotions, recognition, or someone else to define what comes next.

Progress does not arrive as permission. It begins the moment you decide to treat your path as something you design, not something you inherit.

Seeds, Soil, and Growth

Most professionals are taught to chase job titles, periodically polish their résumés, and hope performance speaks for itself. That's like planting a seed and walking away, expecting it to flourish without water, sunlight, or soil.

Left alone, a seed might sprout—but it bends toward whatever light happens to reach it. Roots stay shallow. Weeds crowd in. Growth stalls.

A career works the same way. If you don't actively tend it, someone else will, and usually in ways that serve their priorities, not yours.

Thriving requires intention:

- Water through skill-building
- Sunlight through visibility

- Soil through relationships and networks that anchor and nourish growth

A career isn't a potted plant in the corner. It's a living system that demands care, attention, and adaptation.

From Ladders to Ecosystems

Careers don't grow on ladders. They grow in ecosystems.

Ladders suggest predictability—one rung at a time, climbing steadily in a fixed structure. But work no longer operates that way, and neither do careers.

Ecosystems are nonlinear and alive. Growth isn't always vertical. Sometimes it's lateral into a new function, diagonal into a stretch role, or even a step back to regroup before moving forward again.

The healthiest trees don't just grow upward; they branch, spread, and intertwine. They survive storms because their roots run deep and their structures remain flexible.

Careers follow the same pattern. The question isn't just

How do I climb?

It's also:

Where do I fit? How do I adapt?

How do I thrive while shaping my own growth?

Why Ecosystems Endure

The corporate ladder once made sense in a world of predictability and steady promotion cycles. Today, ladders are fragile. They lean against walls you didn't choose and can disappear through restructuring, automation, or market shifts. Even if you do reach the top, it doesn't guarantee alignment with your values and passions.

Ecosystems endure because they reward resilience over rigidity. Growth comes from reading the environment, finding opportunities, and adapting with intention.

The professionals who thrive long-term aren't chasing rungs. They're building momentum.

The PathFinder Cycle

In ecosystems, growth compounds. It's cyclical, not linear.

That's why this book introduces the PathFinder Cycle—a repeatable framework you'll return to throughout your career. It isn't a rigid blueprint; it's a flywheel. At first, it feels slow. But with each turn, the energy builds. The more you cycle through it, the stronger your momentum becomes.

The five stages of the PathFinder Cycle are:

- **Absorb** — Watch, listen, and learn deeply before you leap

- **Apply** — Turn insight into visible impact

- **Evolve** — Stretch skills, refine identity, and navigate seasons of growth and recovery

- **Elevate** — Make value visible and transition from doer to trusted builder

- **Amplify** — Pay it forward so others succeed because of you

This isn't a ladder you climb. It's a flywheel you spin. Each turn compounds your experience, credibility, and confidence.

Over time, the momentum that you've built becomes your greatest advantage.

From Flywheels to DNA

Careers don't exist in isolation from life. An early mentor once described work and life as a visual depiction of two strands of DNA.

Some seasons demand more from work. Others require life to lead—be it family, health, or personal priorities. Balance isn't equal weight every day; it's knowing which strand must lead in each season without breaking the whole.

PathFinders understand this rhythm. They stretch without snapping, pause without guilt, and pivot without apology.

The Daily Compass of Learning

At the core of it all is a simple philosophy: learn something new every day.

Some days you learn what to do. Most days, you learn what not to do. Either way, learning compounds.

That habit becomes career capital—the credibility that fuels opportunity, especially when the path forward isn't obvious.

Agency, Then Leadership

The most important shift isn't in skills or résumés—it's in mindset:

I will succeed. The only question is whether it happens with you, or in spite of you.

That isn't arrogance. It's agency—the refusal to let your trajectory depend on a single boss, role, or decision.

As you grow in your career, the question evolves:

Do others succeed because of me, or in spite of me?

That's the leadership test. Titles fade. The systems you improve, the friction you remove, and the people you lift are what endure.

A Personal Moment: The Napkin Role

Careers often turn on moments you don't see coming.

One of mine arrived during a routine call when my leader at the time asked if I would shape the future of a product business unit that wasn't yet profitable. There was no plan, just a quick question mark on a napkin while we were both on different calls.

I didn't have all the answers, nor did I fully know what I was stepping into. But I said Yes!

That decision opened opportunities I couldn't have scripted—ability to influence business strategy, turning around a business unit to make it profitable, and building self-credibility across the organization.

Opportunity doesn't wait until you feel ready. But preparation compounds quietly in the background.

A Leadership Snapshot in Practice

Momentum accelerates when strengths and weaknesses are understood—both yours and your team's.

Early in my leadership journey, I inherited a team unsettled by reorganization and a shift in operating model. Instead of rushing into metrics and decisions, I spent a lot of the initial time with the team observing, listening, and resetting expectations. The task at hand was clear: no one had to prove themselves to me; together we had to prove ourselves to the business.

Once roles were aligned with strengths and systems were developed that supported existing gaps, the team's execution accelerated overnight—not because we worked harder, but because we worked with leverage and with a common goal.

Ecosystems reward awareness. Absorbing before applying creates momentum.

The Cost of Drifting

If you don't engage with your ecosystem, you drift.

Drifting looks like staying in roles too long without stretching, letting others define your narrative, confusing busyness with progress, or chasing titles instead of capabilities.

The cost is invisibility when opportunity appears.

Intentional engagement through observing, learning, contributing, and positioning is what creates traction. Credibility begins to travel beyond your title.

Why This Book

Too many professionals are still handed ladders in a world without walls to lean against. They're told to work harder or network more without learning how to turn jobs into careers.

I wrote this book because I have experienced the consequences of both drifting and momentum. Opportunities often arrived before I felt ready—but preparation made them survivable.

This isn't a book of theory. It's a practical framework for building career momentum.

A Way Forward

This book won't promise shortcuts. It offers something more durable: a repeatable system for turning any role into a career that grows with you.

You'll learn how to craft narratives, build visibility without noise, identify whitespace, pace yourself through seasons, and amplify impact beyond yourself.

You are not just another name in the system. You are part of an ecosystem.

When you learn to Absorb, Apply, Evolve, Elevate, and Amplify, you stop drifting—and start shaping the environment around you.

The PathFinder Cycle

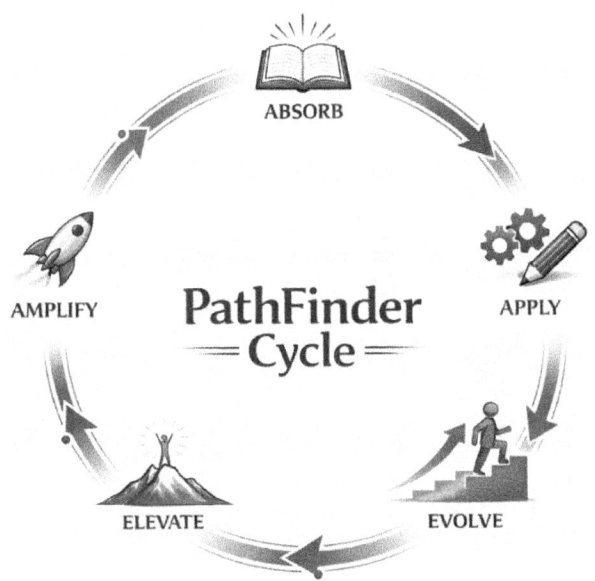

This is not a ladder you climb.
It is a flywheel you return to.

ABSORB

Learn the terrain before
you try to change it.

CHAPTER 1: RETHINKING THE RÉSUMÉ

You are not a list.

Anyone can list tasks. Few articulate value.

A résumé is more than an application document—it's the signal that invites someone to lean in without conveying the whole story, but enough to make them want to learn more. When you shift from listing tasks to signaling trajectory, your résumé stops blending in with others and instead starts setting you apart.

The Illusion of the Perfect Résumé

Résumés have long been treated as golden tickets: polish them, keyword-optimize them, and the next opportunity will magically appear.

Today, with generative AI résumé builders, you can generate one in minutes.

But the reality is, if anyone can do it, then everyone will.

Recruiters now describe drowning in sameness. Dozens of résumés arrive perfectly formatted, identically phrased, and filled with overused verbs like *managed, supported,* or *collaborated.*

Summaries blur together: *Results-driven professional with strong communication skills.*

They're technically flawless but also lifeless.

The differentiator isn't polish. It's narrative.

No one hires a list of tasks. They hire someone who solves problems and creates momentum.

Beyond Job Hunts: A Tool for Any Career Season

Whether you're launching your first search, pivoting industries, or feeling stalled, your résumé is more than an application tool—it's a mirror and a compass.

It reflects where you've been and helps orient where you're going.

You don't update a résumé only when changing jobs. You revisit it to understand your evolution. When momentum slows or direction feels unclear, rewriting your résumé is often the fastest way to reconnect daily work to long-term trajectory.

Why Résumés Fail

Most résumés fall short for three reasons:

- **They're lists, not stories.**
  "Managed projects" tells the recruiter you existed—not that you made a difference.

- **They're written for machines, not humans.**
  Applicant tracking systems reward keywords; hiring managers scan for meaning.

- **They're indistinguishable.**
  If your résumé could describe anyone with your title, you'll be treated like anyone with your title.

The fix is simple but not easy: a résumé that signals your trajectory—the story only you can tell.

13

What Hiring Managers Actually Look For

I've sat on both sides of the table—the candidate hoping to stand out, and the manager skimming résumés late at night after a long day.

Here's what hiring managers actually look for:

- **Clarity** in the first ten seconds

- **Proof of impact** through numbers, outcomes, results

- **A pattern of growth**, not recycled tasks

- **Signals or signs of fit** with the problems at hand

Buzzwords don't create confidence in the hiring manager. Clarity of thought does.

The Résumé as a Narrative

Think of your résumé as the trailer for your career, not the whole movie, but enough to make someone want more.

Each bullet should answer two questions:

- What problem did I solve?

- What momentum did I create?

Below are a couple of examples of framing a bullet point on your résumé

Weak:
Managed a team of five engineers.

Stronger:

Led a team of five engineers to launch an automated testing system that cut in-line defects 40% in six months.

One describes job responsibility. The other describes impact.

Design vs. Substance

Some candidates try to stand out with graphics or creative formatting. The problem is simple: many automated systems can't read them, and managers don't have time to decode them.

Clean and crisp almost always beats flashy.

If you want to showcase design flair, use a portfolio or personal site alongside your profile. Your résumé's sole job is the clarity and context it provides.

A Living Document

Your résumé isn't something you "finish." It's a living document.

Updating it annually forces reflection:

- Did my work tie to meaningful impact?
- Did I build competencies that strengthen my value?
- Does my résumé still reflect where I'm headed?

If you can't add one or two compelling bullets each year, it's not a résumé problem, it's a growth signal.

Instead of drifting through tasks, you must choose work worth documenting. That's how a résumé becomes a career compass.

Case Snapshot: Reframing for Trajectory

I once had someone reach out asking how to break into the MedTech manufacturing industry. Their background was in semiconductor fabrication, leading high-volume fab operations. The challenge wasn't capability. It was translation from one industry to another.

The pivot was not to invent new experiences, but to reframe existing ones into language that resonated inside a different ecosystem.

When we started, their résumé read:

- Managed 24/7 semiconductor fabrication operations across lithography and etch processes

- Led yield improvement initiatives reducing wafer scrap by 18%

- Oversaw equipment uptime and preventive maintenance for Class 1 cleanroom environments

The profile was accurate; the metrics were clearly articulated, but they were also very industry-specific.

We reframed it to:

- Directed 24/7 high-volume manufacturing operations within regulated cleanroom environments

- Spearheaded cross-functional process optimization initiatives reducing defect-related waste by 18%

- Strengthened equipment reliability and production continuity through preventive maintenance and reliability engineering

Same scale. Same outcomes. But an entirely different signal.

The experience didn't change. The results didn't change. Only the language did.

Within weeks, they were interviewing for product-facing manufacturing roles in MedTech—not because they had suddenly become qualified or because they upskilled overnight, but because their capabilities were now visible in the right context.

That's what reframing does. It doesn't alter your achievements, and it doesn't inflate your trajectory. It clarifies both. With each reframing, activity turns into momentum.

You Are Not Your Title

Two people with the same title can leave entirely different legacies. One builds systems intentionally and develops people along the journey. The other checks boxes along the way, hoping for the next list to appear before them.

Your résumé isn't about what you were hired to do. It's about what you actually did in those roles. That's the snapshot that hiring managers look for.

The Through Line

Across every role in your résumé, there's a pattern that develops—a through line that reveals what you bring to the table consistently.

Examples a recruiter recognizes immediately:

- Efficiency builder

- People developer

- Innovation under constraints

- Customer advocate

- Calm in chaos

When your résumé highlights that thread, it stops reading like a list of jobs and starts reading like a career with direction.

Productive PathFinder Practice: Sharpening Your Signal

Your résumé doesn't improve through urgency. It improves through consistency.

Use this framework before you hit "Apply" on the next job application—and once a year regardless of whether you're job searching.

1. Audit for Impact

Rewrite every "Responsible for…" into a PAR story (Problem → Action → Result).

Then strengthen at least one bullet per role with a measurable outcome.

Ask yourself: Does this line show progress or just activity?

2. Remove the Noise

Cut one buzzword per section. If a phrase could describe anyone with your title, replace it with language that reflects how you created momentum within that role.

Clarity beats polish. Specificity beats buzzword adjectives.

3. Clarify Your Direction

Add a two to three sentence narrative or summary statement at the top:

How do you think?

What problems do you solve best?

Where are you headed?

This isn't a summary of your past. It's a signal of trajectory and that growth career you are slowly cultivating.

4. Identify the Through Line

Look across your last three roles. What pattern keeps showing up?

Efficiency builder?

People developer?

Innovation under constraints?

Calm in chaos?

If you can't see a thread, your résumé won't either and neither will the recruiter.

5. Make It a Habit

Set a yearly reminder to refresh your résumé—even if you aren't applying anywhere actively.

If you can't add at least one compelling, impact-driven bullet in a year, that's not a résumé issue. It may signal stagnation.

PathFinder Reflection

- What story is your résumé saying out loud right now?

- Does it signal where you're headed or only where you've been?

- Could someone unknown grasp your value in ten seconds?

- What season of your career does it reveal, and what season do you want it to signal next?

Your résumé isn't static. It's your signal in the noise—both a mirror for reflection and a map for momentum.

CHAPTER 2: CRACKING THE HIDDEN JOB MARKET

Opportunity flows through people, not postings.

You don't need more job boards. You need better conversations.

Most people look for opportunities in the same places, using the same tools, at the same time as everyone else. Truth is careers rarely move through crowded channels. They move through trust, timing, and quiet rooms where roles take shape long before they ever appear online.

Once you understand how opportunity circulates, you stop chasing listings and start positioning yourself where doors open naturally.

Where the Real Jobs Live

Most professionals search in the wrong place.

They polish résumés, refine keywords, and refresh job boards, believing visibility equals opportunity. But the most meaningful roles are rarely public. They're discussed before they're defined, shaped before they're posted.

Before a company advertises a role, someone almost always asks a quieter question:

Do we already know someone who could do this?

If your name surfaces in that moment, you're already inside the conversation.

If it doesn't, you enter later—through a portal, an algorithm, and a stack of identical résumés.

Opportunity doesn't flow through postings. It flows through people.

A Side Door Story

While in graduate school, I was searching for a summer internship. I thought I had done everything right. I polished my résumé the previous fall, attended every career fair, submitted applications to every portal that would accept one.

None of it led anywhere.

I wasn't discouraged. I had simply made peace with it and shifted my focus back to the semester ahead.

Then things changed overnight.

On campus, I ran into a professor I had worked with a few semesters earlier. We scheduled time to catch up over coffee. In the course of conversation, he learned I was still searching for an internship. He mentioned an early-career colleague who was building a small engineering venture and looking for an intern.

Three short conversations later, I had the offer—and one of the most formative summers of my early career.

The internship was never posted. It never appeared on a job board. If I hadn't run into that professor, I likely never would have known it existed.

That experience reframed everything.

Not all opportunities are discovered through applications. Some are unlocked through proximity. Others are created in conversations you didn't plan for.

Side doors often open quietly—but they change trajectories all the same.

Networking vs. Connecting

We've been taught to network. But networking often feels transactional—collecting contacts, trading favors, making asks before trust exists.

Connecting is different.

Connecting is slower. It starts with curiosity rather than need. It's grounded in learning, not extraction.

Instead of asking,

Can you help me find a job?

Try asking,

I'm learning how people build meaningful careers in this field. What shaped your path?

That shift changes the dynamic. People are far more willing to help someone who shows up prepared, thoughtful, and genuinely interested.

Networking collects contacts. Connecting builds trust.

Connection doesn't end when the conversation does.

Follow-through is what turns curiosity into credibility. It's the note you send afterward, the article you promised to share, the update weeks later that shows you listened and remembered.

Anyone can have a good conversation. Few close the loop. And the people who do are the ones who stay top of mind when opportunity begins to take shape.

Trust is the real currency of opportunity.

Three Career Conversations That Matter

Not every conversation needs to be formal. But every conversation benefits from intention.

1. Informational Conversations

Explore how someone entered the field, what surprised them, and what they would do differently. Listen for patterns, not positions.

2. Insider Conversations

Before applying, talk with people who know the work from the inside. Ask about challenges, culture, and what actually drives success.

3. Value-Driven Conversations

Don't only ask for help. Offer insight. Share something relevant. Contribute perspective based on what you've learned.

Each type of conversation expands the ecosystem you grow within.

The conversation opens the door. Follow-through keeps it open.

Why This Works

Opportunity moves through relationships because relationships reduce risk. When trust exists, uncertainty shrinks. And when uncertainty shrinks, doors open earlier.

Often, it isn't your closest relationships that matter most. It's the looser connections that bridge you into new contexts, new teams, and new conversations. These ties expand your field of view beyond what you already know.

This is why people hear about roles before they're posted, or shape opportunities that didn't exist before a conversation began.

Common Pitfalls

- **Spray-and-Pray Applications** — sending dozens of applications without human connection feels productive but produces little traction.
- **One-Sided Asks** — reaching out only when you need something erodes trust quickly.
- **Ignoring Weak Ties** — former colleagues, classmates, or second-degree connections are often the bridges to new opportunities.
- **No Follow-Through** — treating a single conversation as a finish line instead of a starting point. Momentum comes from staying present after the meeting ends.

Every missed follow-through is a seed left untended.

Productive PathFinder Practice: Your Opportunity Map

Create three lists:

1. People You Know

Peers, former colleagues, mentors, leaders.

2. People You'd Like to Know

Operators, thinkers, and builders doing work you respect.

3. People You Can Help

Because value shared often finds its way back.

Now set a simple goal:

Reach out to three people this week—thoughtfully, not transactionally.

Keep it human. Ask thoughtful question, then Listen. Most importantly follow through.

Momentum isn't built by luck. It's built through deliberate conversation.

PathFinder Reflection

Think about your last job move.

Did you apply cold through a portal, or did someone know your name before the role existed?

If it was cold, what one action could make it warmer next time?

A message.

A comment.

A coffee.

An introduction.

A useful insight.

A follow-up that shows you meant what you said.

Each one is a seed.

And seeds only grow when placed in soil that supports them—relationships, alignment, reciprocity, and trust.

Careers don't grow through clicks.

They grow through connection—and connection is sustained through follow-through.

Because most jobs aren't posted.

They're proposed.

And proposals happen in rooms where trust already exists.

CHAPTER 3: FIRST IMPRESSIONS, FAST WINS

How credibility begins before influence

Be a signal, not noise.

The first 90 days in a new job or new role aren't about proving everything. They're about proving the right things—steadiness, curiosity, and relevance. In every new environment, people make quiet, lasting judgments about you long before they fully understand what you're capable of.

This chapter focuses on shaping that impression intentionally: not through volume, but through reliability; not through ambition, but through execution.

Why the First 90 Days Matter

Your first weeks don't just set the tone. They shape the story others tell about you long after results arrive.

In every transition—whether it's your first job, a return after a pause, a pivot into a new field, or a leadership promotion—expectations reset. People watch for subtle signals:

Are you dependable?

Curious?

Coachable?

Adaptive?

You don't need a grand entrance to build credibility. You need to become someone others can trust to deliver.

Confidence without arrogance.

Action without noise.

Presence without pressure.

Your goal isn't to get everything accomplished. It's to become a reliable asset to the team and organization.

Loud vs. Lasting

Early in my career, a new leader joined our team. He was quiet and unassuming, but there was a determination in how he approached his work.

For the first few weeks, there were no dramatic declarations, no challenges to long-standing practices, no public corrections. Just observation. Listening. Copious note-taking.

Then something shifted.

His questions grew sharper. His thinking became more defined. His vision clearer. He began outlining a bold operating model for the team and site—not from impulse, but from understanding.

Because he had taken the time to absorb the people, the processes, and the reasons systems existed as they did, he changed things from a position of strength.

The team bought in easily. Credibility had already been built before influence was ever exercised.

Around that same time, a friend told me about a leader newly hired into his organization. Highly credentialed and recruited from a competitor. Confident from day one.

In his first week, he spoke in every meeting. He challenged long-standing processes. He proposed sweeping changes before fully understanding why the existing systems were in place.

When invited to walk the floor and observe the workflow, he responded,

"I'm not here to see things. I'm here to fix them."

At first, people admired the energy.

Within a month, they began tuning him out. Within three months, many of the team, including my friend—had left.

His words outpaced his understanding. His confidence outpaced his context. His credibility eroded faster than his ideas arrived.

Same environment. Same opportunity window.

Two capable professionals. Only one earned influence.

The difference wasn't intelligence. It was signal versus noise.

Execution, not volume—determines who gets to be remembered.

Decode the Culture Before You Disrupt It

Every workplace has an unwritten rulebook.

Pay attention to:

- Who speaks and more importantly who gets heard

- How quickly do people respond

- How conflict is handled

- What gets celebrated

- Which behaviors are tolerated

- Where informal influence lives

Before trying to change the system, understand it.

Respecting context doesn't mean conforming. It means earning the right to improve what exists.

Look for Small, Strategic Wins

A fast win isn't flashy. It's useful.

Look for:

- Important work no one owns

- Bottlenecks everyone tolerates

- Recurring tasks done inconsistently

- Gaps where clarity would change everything

I once had a team member join our manufacturing setup. Within her first few weeks, she noticed inconsistencies in how the team operated.

The shop floor lacked organization. Each shift set up the workspace differently. There were no structured pass-down notes between shifts. Information was lost at handoff. Problems were rediscovered instead of resolved.

She didn't make speeches about inefficiency. She didn't criticize the system.

She volunteered to create a simple pass-down template— a structured way to document key updates from one shift to the next. Nothing complex. Just clarity.

Over time, communication improved.

Efficiency increased. Order returned to the floor.

It was a small intervention. But it was a powerful signal.

Her reliability became synonymous with order. Within months, she was coordinating cross-functional optimization projects—not because she asked for visibility, but because she consistently delivered trust.

Small wins create trust. Trust creates access. Access creates opportunity.

Noise vs. Credibility

In the rush to impress, people fall into predictable traps:

- Over-speaking

- Over-promising

- Offering solutions before understanding the problem

- Trying to be impressive instead of useful

Energy opens doors. Reliability keeps them open.

Deliver first. Then, when you speak, people listen.

Common Pitfalls

- Trying to prove everything at once
- Talking before listening
- Waiting silently instead of contributing
- Chasing recognition too early
- Confusing activity with impact

These behaviors feel productive in the moment. They quietly erode trust over time.

Productive PathFinder Practice: Map Your Fast Win

Ask yourself:

1. What's one recurring issue your team complains about but tolerates?
2. What's one task that falls through the cracks because no one owns it?
3. What's one small improvement you could deliver on in the next 30 days?

Choose one. Own it. Deliver it consistently.

Credibility begins with deliberate usefulness.

Why This Works

Trust compounds like interest. The earlier you invest, the more it works for you later.

You don't demand trust. You earn it by:

- Showing up prepared
- Staying curious without judgment
- Doing what you said you would
- Admitting what you don't know
- Following through consistently

By the time a larger opportunity appears, trust will have already positioned you.

Trust isn't a title.

It's a reputation built over time and reinforced daily.

PathFinder Reflection

Think about your most recent transition.

What signals did you send in your first weeks – noise or reliability?

Where could you trade visibility for usefulness? What small commitment could you lead and deliver consistently right now?

Credibility isn't built through big moments. It's built through kept promises.

Ideas attract attention. Execution sustains it.

The professionals who rise aren't the loudest. They're the most dependable.

Execution speaks first. Influence follows.

APPLY

Turn insight into motion
through small steps, taken early

CHAPTER 4:
OPPORTUNITY MAPPING

Seeing the terrain before others do.

Don't wait for the path to appear. Learn to read the terrain.

Execution earns trust. But eventually, execution alone stops being enough. Once reliability is established, what differentiates momentum from stagnation is not effort—it's awareness.

Opportunity mapping is the shift from reacting to anticipating. From completing tasks to noticing patterns. From following the playbook to recognizing where it no longer fits.

This chapter is about developing the habit that separates dependable contributors from emergent leaders: seeing what others overlook—and acting with restraint and discipline.

From Execution to Anticipation

Execution builds credibility, while Anticipation builds trajectory.

Early in any role, people look for dependability. Soon after, they expect initiative. Eventually, they rely on insight—the ability to sense what's coming and respond before the system demands it.

Opportunity mapping is the hinge between those stages. It's how professionals move from waiting for direction to shaping it quietly.

The people who advance fastest are rarely the loudest. They're the ones who see one move ahead.

Seeing What Others Miss

Most people experience their job as a list of tasks. PathFinders experience it as an ecosystem — one that is interconnected, imperfect, and full of signals.

Those signals often sound like:

- "This always slows us down."

- "We've tried fixing this before."

- "It's temporary."

- "That's just how it works."

These aren't annoyances. They're information.

Every inefficiency points to unclaimed responsibility. Every recurring frustration reveals a gap in ownership. Every workaround is an invitation for someone willing to step in thoughtfully.

A Story of Stepping In

During graduate school, I worked part-time in tech support. On paper, the role was simple. We followed a scripted set of diagnostic questions as first-level support. If the issue wasn't resolved, we escalated it to the full-time staff.

Over time, I noticed a pattern. I was escalating eight out of ten calls each day. The engineering team was backing up, and callers were left frustrated. To add to it, once a ticket was escalated, we rarely learned what the actual issue or resolution had been.

So, we kept escalating—without learning.

I quietly began mapping the types of issues being passed upstream. Over several weeks, I cataloged recurring patterns. The same categories surfaced repeatedly.

Instead of accepting it as "just the process," I brought the data to my supervisor with a simple proposal: If we received targeted training on the most common escalation categories, we could resolve more issues at first level—reducing backlog and improving response time.

Leadership agreed to test it.

Within a month of implementation, first-level resolution rates increased from 20% to 60%.

Engineering backlog decreased.

Caller satisfaction improved.

Team morale lifted.

I didn't have the title to fix the system. I didn't have the authority to rewrite workflows.

I mapped the gap, identified a pattern and proposed a solution.

Over time, I was entrusted with broader responsibilities— not because I asked for them, but because I had demonstrated I could improve the system, not just execute within it.

Whitespace problems aren't distractions.

They're leverage points.

The Whitespace Advantage

Every organization has whitespace. Most people avoid it.

Whitespace shows up as:

- Processes everyone tolerates but no one updates
- Responsibilities that "don't belong to anyone"
- Communication gaps between teams
- Systems that work—until they don't
- Data without clear ownership

Stepping into whitespace doesn't mean claiming territory. It means offering clarity. Curiosity instead of criticism. Support instead of control.

Over time, a pattern forms: things run smoother when you're involved.

Common Pitfalls

Opportunity mapping requires restraint. Watch for these traps:

- **Overreaching too early** — proposing large changes without context
- **Naming problems without solutions** — visibility without contribution

- **Trying to fix everything** — breadth without impact

- **Claiming solo credit** — influence grows faster when shared

Opportunity mapping isn't about doing more. It's about seeing better.

Productive PathFinder Practice: Build Your Opportunity Map

Use this practice to turn observation into action:

1. **Notice the Friction**

   For two weeks, write down recurring inefficiencies or normalized frustrations.

2. **Talk to the System**

   Ask two or three people involved. Listen for patterns, not fault.

3. **Pilot One Fix**

   Design a small, reversible improvement—something that takes days to implement, not months.

4. **Close the Loop**

   Share what changed and what improved.

Consistency here builds a quiet reputation: things work better when you're involved.

PathFinder Reflection

- What frustration has my team normalized?

- What patterns am I seeing but not acting on?

- What's the smallest fix I could pilot this month?

- What whitespace have I been avoiding—and why?

The best opportunities aren't assigned. They're discovered.

Opportunity rarely announces itself. It hides in handoffs, workarounds, and gaps no one owns. The professionals who build lasting momentum don't wait for clarity—they create it carefully.

Seeing the terrain is the first step. Shaping it comes next.

CHAPTER 5: PROACTIVE CAREER DESIGN

Stop climbing. Start shaping.

If you don't design your career, someone else will—usually around their goals, not yours.

Most careers don't stall because people lack ambition. They stall because people follow paths they didn't choose.

They climb the ladder placed in front of them. They say yes to the first visible role. They chase titles because titles are measurable and socially validated.

But ladders are dangerous when they lean against the wrong wall.

A career isn't something to climb. It's something to design—intentionally, deliberately, in alignment with who you are becoming.

Waiting to be chosen isn't a strategy. It's drift disguised as progress.

If you don't design your direction, someone else will. And their blueprint rarely optimizes for your growth.

Stop Climbing, Start Shaping

Once you see the terrain, the next step is about choosing where to go.

Execution earns trust. Opportunity mapping reveals leverage. But without direction, momentum becomes motion without meaning. At a certain point, the question isn't *Can I deliver?* It's *Am I building toward the right work?*

Proactive career design is the shift from reacting to openings to shaping your trajectory—before the next title, before the next reorg, before the next "should."

When "Next" Isn't Better

I once worked with a colleague who was determined to climb at every opportunity. They were the first to raise their hand for internal openings and just as active in building external visibility.

Eventually, the effort paid off. They were offered an external role at a significantly higher level.

It looked like progress.

Some peers quietly wondered whether it was a step too soon—whether the scope and expectations would outpace the support system that had helped them succeed.

Within six months, the excitement faded.

The new role demanded constant administrative oversight, stakeholder alignment, and political navigation. What had once been energizing execution became calendar management and conflict resolution.

They weren't unqualified. They were misaligned.

The step up wasn't wrong—it was premature.

Exhaustion set in. Frustration followed. Burnout wasn't the result of incompetence. It was the result of chasing the symbol of success instead of the substance of work.

A few years later, I had the privilege of working with another teammate facing a similar opportunity. This time, the choice looked different.

Instead of pursuing the first available promotion, they expanded their scope from within. They volunteered for a cross-functional initiative. They built execution repeatability. They mentored new hires. They quietly resolved a recurring process inefficiency.

Their visibility increased—not because they chased it, but because their work made the team stronger.

A year later, during an organizational reshuffle, a leadership role opened. They were unanimously chosen.

This time, the step up fit their strengths, their energy, and their trajectory.

One person climbed. The other designed.

Success isn't about moving up. It's about moving toward the right work.

Spotlight: The Slow Burn Advantage

Impatience derails more careers than lack of skill.

When you're early on your journey, visibility feels urgent. Prestige feels important. Recognition feels validating.

But momentum built too quickly can lead to misalignment.
Momentum built slowly through depth, credibility, and clarity, is what endures.

Being overlooked today doesn't mean you're stuck. It might mean you're laying the foundation for a leap that actually aligns with who you want to become.

Slow doesn't mean stagnant. Slow can mean being strategic.

Design Like a Builder

The most effective career designers think like builders. They ask three questions before they commit to a path:

1. Who benefits most from my best work?

Not who applauds it, but who actually gains value when you show up at your best.

2. What problems energize me?

Not what you're capable of, but what you want to keep doing when it gets hard.

3. What skills will matter in the world I'm moving into?

Not the skills that earned yesterday's promotion, the skills that will earn tomorrow's options.

Those questions move you from reaction to intention. Your career stops being a series of assignments and starts becoming a direction you can defend.

Prototype, Don't Overplan

Forget rigid five-year plans. They collapse under real-world change.

PathFinders don't rely on perfect plans. They rely on learning loops.

Prototype your next step with small, low-risk experiments:

- Shadow someone in another function
- Volunteer to lead a contained initiative
- Pilot a tool or workflow improvement
- Take on a low-risk, high-learning assignment
- Mentor a junior colleague or onboard a new hire
- Join a cross-functional tiger team

Each experiment teaches you something:

- What energizes you
- What drains you
- Where you add the most value
- What you need to learn next
- Which environments amplify your strengths

You don't need certainty. You need cadence. Small experiments create big clarity.

Stretch Inside the Role You Have

You don't need a new title to grow. Some of the most meaningful development happens long before anyone changes your job description.

Stretch your current scope by:

- Taking on a recurring problem

51

- Mentoring or onboarding others

- Leading a small internal project end-to-end

- Becoming the "go-to" person for a specific competency

These moves prove something stronger than ambition. They prove readiness.

Your current role becomes your lab for building the next version of you—all done without waiting for permission or a posted opening.

Why This Works

When people drift, it rarely looks like it is drifting. It often looks like being busy. It looks like being dependable. It looks like being the person who always says yes.

But design changes the signal.

Instead of being the most available, you become the most intentional. Instead of collecting responsibilities, you compound capability. Instead of chasing visibility, you earn it through work that aligns with direction.

Design invites growth.

Drift invites regret.

Common Pitfalls

Career drift often hides behind productivity. Watch for these traps:

- **Chasing titles blindly** — landing the wrong role for the wrong reasons

- **Overengineering the plan** — planning endlessly without experimenting

- **Waiting to be chosen** — letting others dictate your direction

- **Ignoring core values** — taking roles misaligned with how you work best

- **Mistaking activity for progress** — confusing movement with momentum

Drift isn't failure. Drift is feedback. It simply shows where intention is missing.

Productive PathFinder Practice: Design Your Next 90 Days

Create three columns:

- What I Do Today

- What I Want More Of

- Adjacent Growth Opportunities

Fill them in honestly. Then choose one 90-day experiment that is small, meaningful, and measurable.

At the end of 90 days, ask:

- Did it energize me?

- Did it build credibility?

- Did it align with my direction?

- Should I deepen it, extend it, or pivot?

This is proactive design in motion:

learn → test → refine.

PathFinder Reflection

- Am I reacting to openings and expectations—or shaping my trajectory?

- If I look five years ahead, will I respect the choices I'm making right now?

- Does my current path serve who I am becoming—or who I used to be?

A career isn't a ladder. It's a living system. Shape it like one.

Your career doesn't just happen to you. It is built—through quiet decisions made consistently.

And once direction becomes clear, something else changes.

People begin to look to you—not for your title, but for your clarity.

Influence doesn't wait for hierarchy. It grows where trust and direction intersect.

EVOLVE

Align who you are
with how you grow.

CHAPTER 6: LEADING WITHOUT AUTHORITY

The people who shape your trajectory.

The right people don't just teach you—they accelerate your trajectory.

Careers don't grow in isolation. Behind every outcome or breakthrough is a web of people, some who guide, some who advocate, and some who quietly teach you who not to become.

The truth is simple: no one rises alone.

The professionals who grow the fastest and endure the longest are the ones who learn to cultivate the ecosystem around them.

The Network Beneath the Surface

No tree flourishes alone. Its roots intertwine with others, drawing stability and strength from shared soil.

Your career works the same way.

Mentors, allies, and anti-mentors form the living network that sustains growth. Trying to build a career entirely through self-reliance feels noble, but isolation slows progress. Guidance, trust, and connection act like nutrients in the soil—helping you learn faster, anchor more deeply, and navigate uncertainty with clarity.

When you treat relationships as part of your growth system, you stop networking for opportunity and start building for endurance.

Careers grow in communities.

Momentum tends to accelerate through three types of people:

1. those who develop your thinking
2. those who expand your reach

3. those who clarify your boundaries

Sometimes they arrive intentionally. Sometimes they arrive by contrast.

Mentorship Accelerator

I once worked for a manager who took personal ownership of my career direction. He didn't just assign tasks, instead he built trajectory.

At one point, he arranged for his own manager to mentor me. At the time, it felt slightly uncomfortable. But it became one of the most formative experiences of my career to date.

From my immediate manager, I learned what secure leadership looks like. He was confident enough in his own role that my growth never threatened it. There was no insecurity, no gatekeeping, only clarity, encouragement and leadership.

From his manager, I experienced true mentorship. Not advice delivered casually, but trust extended intentionally. Conversations were confidential and centered on my development—not just the mechanics of the work. The whole experience led to an increase in expectations for performance but ultimately guarded with the highest levels of support.

What stood out most wasn't the guidance itself. It was the alignment. Three levels within an organization working in harmony, ensuring daily responsibilities were executed while deliberately nurturing future leadership.

That's what good mentorship does.

It multiplies momentum.

The Ally Who Won't Let You Hide

A few years later, I sought guidance from outside my organization and began working with a professional career coach.

At first, the conversations felt circular. We would explore goals, barriers, and possibilities—and almost inevitably, the dialogue would end with the same question:

"Okay. What's actually stopping you from asking for the opportunity?"

It felt repetitive. At times, even unproductive. I wondered whether I was investing time in conversations that weren't moving anywhere.

Then, weeks after the engagement ended, it clicked.

They weren't trying to give me answers. They were removing my excuses.

The coach wasn't solving my problem. They were exposing my hesitation.

I had been asking for opportunities in passive ways— waiting for someone to invite me into rooms I wanted to be in. The inaction wasn't lack of access. It was self-doubt.

That realization shifted everything.

I ended up pursuing a certification in nonprofit board governance. I positioned myself intentionally. I initiated conversations instead of waiting for them.

What I had previously described as "no opening available" became "I haven't stepped forward yet."

An ally doesn't clear the path for you. They make it harder for you to hide from it.

The Anti – Mentor

I found myself being a part of a team led by a manager who consistently positioned themselves as the most informed voice in the room.

On the surface, the environment appeared collaborative. Meetings opened with questions. Input was requested. Perspectives were invited.

But over time, a pattern emerged.

Decisions had often been made before the discussion began. Contributions were acknowledged but rarely incorporated. Direction defaulted upward.

The result wasn't immediate conflict. It was gradual disengagement.

When people sense their thinking won't influence outcomes, they stop offering it. When decisions consistently funnel through one voice, development narrows. Progress stalls quietly.

Eventually, team members began leaving or seeking reassignment. Not because they lacked opportunity—but because they lacked ownership.

In hindsight, it was an example of anti-mentoring.

Not overtly harmful. Not intentionally suppressive. But structurally limiting.

Mentorship expands capacity.

Anti-mentoring centralizes it.

The difference isn't intelligence. It's security.

Secure leaders create space for others to think, decide, and stretch. Insecure leadership, even unintentionally, constrains it.

That experience reshaped how I think about growth environments.

A mentor doesn't just share knowledge. They share space.

Mentors: Pattern-Finders, Not Professors

Great mentors don't exist to give instructions. They exist to develop and expand perspective.

A strong mentor helps you see patterns, inflection points, and blind spots you haven't yet learned to recognize. They challenge comfort without crushing confidence. They don't remove complexity—they help you read it.

Mentorship takes many forms:

Formal mentors — Structured programs or assigned pairings. Helpful starting points, though often limited in depth.

Organic mentors — Built through mutual respect, curiosity, and shared work. These are often the most transformative.

Situational mentors — Short-term guides for specific decisions, projects, or transitions.

Waiting for the "perfect mentor" is like waiting for perfect weather. You miss the season you're in.

Mentorship is less about finding the ideal teacher and more about learning to extract insight from every interaction. Preparation and follow-through turn small moments into lasting guidance.

Allies: Quiet Architects of Opportunity

If mentors expand your thinking, allies expand your reach.

Allies advocate for you in rooms you're not in. They share credit, make introductions, and amplify your work without being asked. They are peers, managers, and partners who use influence to open doors.

Allies aren't cheerleaders. They're accelerators.

The foundation of alliance is reciprocity. You build it by celebrating others' wins, offering perspective without keeping score, sharing opportunity, and showing up when pressure is high.

Trust compounds over time. When you invest consistently in others, doors open in ways you could never engineer alone.

Allies transform potential into visibility.

Anti-Mentors: Lessons in Contrast

Some teachers never intended to teach.

The insecure manager who leads through fear. The peer who undermines collaboration. The leader who values credit over impact. The boss who burns trust faster than they build it.

These individuals clarify values by violating them.

Instead of dwelling in frustration, observe with curiosity:

What is it about their approach that damages trust?

Which behaviors create unnecessary friction?

What kind of environment do you want to build or rather avoid?

Anti-mentors sharpen boundaries. They remind you who you refuse to become.

Contrast is a form of clarity.

Common Pitfalls

Growth networks erode quietly when intention fades. Watch for these traps:

- Waiting for formality and missing organic relationships

- Treating mentorship as transactional instead of relational

- Over-relying on one voice until perspective narrows

- Ignoring the lessons hidden in poor role models

- Consuming guidance without contributing your own insights in return

Strong networks aren't built quickly. They're built deliberately.

Productive PathFinder Practice: Map Your Growth Network

Create three lists:

Mentors | Allies | Anti-Mentors

Under each, list:

- Two or three names

- One insight already gained

- One follow-up or expression of gratitude you can offer

- One next action you can take

Then act:

- Ask a mentor for perspective

- Offer an ally support

- Write down what an anti-mentor clarified for you

Growth accelerates when curiosity meets connection.

PathFinder Reflection

Think about your last significant breakthrough.

Who shifted your perspective?

Who opened a door you couldn't open alone?

Who, through contrast, taught you what not to compromise on?

Your answers reveal your growth system, the soil beneath your career.

Which roots need strengthening?

Which relationships need water?

Where should you plant next?

You are responsible for your growth—but not meant to grow alone.

The right mentors sharpen thinking.

The right allies expand reach.

The right anti-mentors clarify boundaries.

Curate them with intention, and your ecosystem will compound momentum long after titles change.

Influence isn't built alone.

It's built in alignment over time.

CHAPTER 7: MASTERING PRODUCTIVE SYSTEMS

Building the structure that sustains your success.

Discipline beats motivation when life gets loud.

Early career momentum often comes from energy. You're new, curious, eager to prove yourself. But as responsibility expands, energy alone stops being enough.

The professionals who sustain excellence long after novelty fades aren't powered by adrenaline.

They're sustained by systems.

Systems aren't the opposite of creativity. They're the infrastructure that protects it.

From Support to Structure

Your network accelerates you. Your systems sustain you.

Growth eventually reaches a threshold where guidance isn't the constraint, but capacity is. You don't need more advice or more potential. You need structure.

A career built only on motivation will sprint — and then stall.
A career built on intentional systems endures.

Systems don't box you in. They create space. They reduce friction, convert ambition into traction, and protect energy from constant decision-making.

Support is how you rise. Structure is how you stay relevant.

Why Systems Matter

Early on, enthusiasm carries the load. You absorb quickly, push through long days, and rely on effort and work ethic to cover gaps.

Then life expands as deadlines multiply.

Expectations compound and personal responsibilities grow.

Your calendar fills with red blocks and reactive work.

At this stage, the professionals who thrive aren't the most motivated. They're the ones who design repeatable workflows that make execution feel natural instead of forced.

Motivation sparks action but systems sustain motion.

Discipline alone doesn't get you there. It's about designing systems where discipline becomes the path of least resistance.

Leader Standard Work: When Structure Creates Clarity

Early in my leadership journey, I was fueled by adrenaline and quietly overwhelmed by it. The more I delivered; the more responsibility arrived. Days began to blur into nights. Meetings overlapped. Emails piled up. Eventually, small commitments began slipping through the cracks.

I wasn't failing. Most things were still getting done.

But I was running on fumes—one or two missteps away from burnout or a poor decision.

At that point, a mentor introduced me to the concept of Leader Standard Work.

The idea was surprisingly simple. Across any day, week, or month, there are certain leadership tasks that repeat, such as reviews, check-ins, planning moments, and follow-ups that trigger work for others. Instead of keeping those obligations in your head, you document them.

A simple checklist.

By mapping those recurring responsibilities, structure replaced mental clutter with clarity. I no longer had to remember everything. The system remembered for me.

With that clarity, my mind shifted from reacting to the present toward preparing for what came next. Instead of scrambling to stay afloat, I could start each day with intention.

Over time, many of those repeatable actions became muscle memory. Others were delegated as the team matured.

But the real lesson stayed with me.

Structure doesn't restrict leadership.

It protects it.

The Friday Reset

As my roles expanded over the years, something else began to disappear: protected thinking time.

Time to step back.

Time to reflect.

Time to work on myself rather than simply working through the next task.

Without realizing it, the calendar had filled with execution but left little space for perspective. The same system that once helped me stay organized now needed to evolve.

So, I repurposed the standard work idea into something new.

I called it the Friday Reset.

Every Friday, I blocked protected time to pause and reset the system around me. The ritual was simple:

- Review ongoing commitments

- Identify the critical priorities for the following week

- Reset expectations with the team where needed

- Clear unnecessary noise

- Create space to think about improvements, ideas, and strategic shifts

It wasn't about productivity. It was about clarity.

Over time, that small ritual shaped my reputation—not through brilliance, but through consistency.

Small systems compound into reliability.

And reliability is what allows leaders to think clearly when complexity rises.

Designing Around Your Rhythm

Productivity isn't about managing time. It's about managing energy.

High performers don't fight their natural rhythm. They design around it.

Protect peak hours for deep work and thinking. Reserve low-energy windows for logistics and admin. Schedule recovery intentionally.

Rest isn't a reward. It's part of the system that enables output.

When your calendar reflects your rhythm instead of ignoring it, work shifts from friction to flow.

Borrow, Build, Break

There is no perfect system. There is only what works for you in the moment.

Systems evolve because roles evolve and life evolves.

Instead of chasing the ideal setup, use a simple loop:

Borrow — Start with something proven.

Build — Adapt it to your context and goals.

Break — Let it go when it no longer fits.

Growth isn't about accumulating more habits.

It's about curating the few that matter today.

Tools change. Principles don't.

Common Pitfalls

Most systems fail not because they're flawed—but because they're brittle.

Watch for these traps:

- Tool chasing instead of clarity

- Over-engineering systems that collapse under pressure

- Rigidity when life demands flexibility

- Ignoring recovery until burnout forces a reset

Strong systems are:

Simple. Adaptable. Repeatable.

That's what lasts.

Productive PathFinder Practice: Audit, Adjust, Anchor

Use this practice to build a system that survives real life:

1. **Audit the friction**

   Where do you feel scattered or reactive?

2. **Adjust one thing**

   Morning planning, weekly review, meeting prep, or nightly shutdown.

3. **Anchor the ritual**

Tie it to a cue—Friday reset, Sunday restart, end-of-day close.

4. **Assess and adapt**

Keep what works. Refine what doesn't. Discard the rest.

The best system isn't perfect. It's the one you still use when things get messy.

PathFinder Reflection

Think of the most dependable person you know.

They aren't magical. They're structured.

Their systems are invisible—but their impact isn't.

Ask yourself: What small structure could I build this month that would make my value easier to trust?

Success isn't sustained by motivation. It's sustained by systems that protect rhythm, focus, and follow-through.

And once your systems are stable, something deeper comes into focus.

Not just *how* you work—but also *why*.

CHAPTER 8: IDENTITY, PURPOSE, AND VALUES

Your inner compass

Without clarity on who you are, no role will ever feel right.

There comes a point in every career where technical skill is no longer the differentiator. You know how to execute. You know how to deliver. You've built credibility and momentum.

And yet, something still feels unsettled.

That discomfort isn't a lack of knowledge or ability. It's a lack of alignment.

When identity, purpose, and values remain undefined, even prestigious roles can feel hollow. Promotions land but don't satisfy. Progress continues but meaning erodes.

This chapter is about developing the inner compass that keeps you grounded when titles shift, responsibilities expand, and the external world grows louder.

Why Identity Matters

Skill opens doors. Identity determines whether you want to walk through them.

Many professionals reach a stage where achievement stops delivering fulfillment. They hit targets, earn recognition, and still feel restless. That restlessness isn't failure, it's feedback.

It signals a growing gap between the work you're doing and the person you're becoming.

Identity answers questions technical skill cannot:

- What kind of work energizes me?
- What kind of leader do I want to be?

- What environments bring out my best?

- What compromise am I unwilling to make?

You can succeed on paper and still feel misaligned in practice.

The antidote isn't a new role. It's clarity.

When Pressure Reveals Identity

I once worked on a project team preparing for a significant product launch. About three weeks before the launch date, the situation suddenly shifted into crisis mode. The project lead and two other key members of the team were unable to continue for various reasons, and what had been a structured plan quickly became uncertainty.

After taking stock of the situation, I brought it to my manager and explained where we stood. His first response was simple. He asked whether we thought we could still get it done.

I told him it would take a lot of long hours, and that we would need a few key people to step in and help stabilize the work.

He paused for a moment and said to give him a few hours while we continued building a recovery plan.

Within a day, one of the conference rooms had been converted into what we jokingly called the *war room*. Whiteboards were filled with timelines, action items, and open problems. He had identified a handful of team members who were known for being doers—people who could step into ambiguity and move things forward.

But the part that stood out most was this: he cleared his own calendar and joined us in the room.

He wasn't directing the effort from a distance. He was down in the trenches with us—helping remove obstacles, checking in on progress, and sometimes simply being present while the team worked through problems.

Over the next two weeks, we unraveled the situation one issue at a time. Long days and late nights became the norm, but the atmosphere in the room never turned heavy. We worked hard, but we also built friendships along the way. One of the new team members even insisted that our manager try coffee boba for the first time, which he did, and just like that a moment was shared within the team that became an inside joke in future meeting settings.

Slowly, the chaos began to stabilize. Problems were solved. Dependencies cleared. The path forward became visible again.

And in the end, we launched on time.

Looking back, a few things stood out from that experience.

First, a leader defining his identity. We could have easily delayed the launch and pointed to the circumstances. Instead, he chose ownership. More importantly, he rolled up his sleeves and joined the team in the work—even if sometimes only as a steady presence and a source of encouragement.

Second, the room developed a shared purpose. Many of the people who stepped in had not worked on the project before. But over those two weeks, the goal became collective. It was no longer about individual responsibilities. It was about delivering something together.

Experiences like that stay with you over the course of a career. They shape how you think about leadership, teamwork, and responsibility.

Because identity isn't something leaders declare in calm moments.

It's something teams discover through how you show up when things get hard.

Values Reveal the Season You're In

During a leadership workshop, I once sat across from a senior leader while we were working through a core values identification exercise. The activity required us to narrow a long list of possible values down to just two cards that represented what mattered most.

When the exercise ended, we shared our selections with the group.

Interestingly, both of us had chosen Family as our first value.

For the second card, however, our choices diverged.

I had selected Lifelong Learning. He had chosen Leaving a Legacy.

During the lunch break, we found ourselves talking about the "why" behind those choices.

My reasoning was straightforward. I was still early in my career, learning, exploring, and trying to understand how the different pieces of leadership and life fit together. Growth felt like the most natural value to anchor to at the time.

His answer carried a different perspective.

After a couple of decades of leadership, he was thinking less about what he still needed to learn and more about what he could pass forward. His focus had shifted toward ensuring the knowledge, experience, and lessons from his journey would benefit the next generation of leaders.

That conversation stayed with me.

Values often reveal the season you're in.

Early in a career, they tend to center around growth and exploration. Later, they often shift toward contribution and impact.

Neither is better than the other.

They simply reflect where you are in that season of life—and more importantly, who you're becoming.

Over time, values become quiet decision filters. They influence the work you pursue, the environments you choose, and the kind of leader you decide to be.

Identity: Who You're Becoming

Identity is not your title. It isn't your role or your résumé.

It's the internal narrative you carry about who you are and who you're becoming.

Ask yourself:

- What am I known for today?

- What do I want to be known for three years from now?

- If I lost my title tomorrow, what part of me would remain?

Identity built on external validation collapses under pressure.

Identity built on values, strengths, and lived experience endures.

Organizations define roles. You define identity.

Purpose: Why You Show Up

Purpose doesn't need to be grand. It needs to be honest.

Purpose is the reason you continue when work gets difficult. It's what gives effort meaning and makes friction tolerable.

Purpose can sound like:

- I want to keep learning.

- I want to build stability for my family.

- I want to reduce unnecessary complexity.

- I want to create opportunities for others.

Purpose doesn't eliminate challenge. It provides the context for the challenge.

Without purpose, achievement feels hollow.

With purpose, even hard seasons feel worthwhile.

Values: Your Boundaries

Values are the guardrails that protect you from drift.

They guide decisions when trade-offs appear and pressure increases. They help you say:

- no without guilt

- yes without hesitation

- not yet without confusion

Examples include integrity, curiosity, impact, balance, or service—but the words matter less than the clarity behind them.

When values are undefined, decisions default to fear, urgency, or approval-seeking. When values are clear, choices feel aligned—even when they're difficult.

Values don't limit your options.

They define your path.

Common Pitfalls

Drift rarely looks reckless. It looks responsible.

Watch for these patterns:

- Letting titles define worth

- Borrowing someone else's purpose

- Saying yes out of obligation instead of alignment

- Staying busy without reflection

- Mistaking success for fulfillment

Drift isn't failure. It's feedback—showing where clarity is missing.

Productive PathFinder Practice: Write Your Compass

Use this exercise to anchor your direction:

1. **Identity statement**

   Write two or three sentences about who you're becoming—independent of title.

2. **Purpose sentence**

   Complete: *I show up each day because…*

3. **Values list**

   Identify five values. Circle the three you won't compromise.

4. **Decision test**

   Apply these to one upcoming choice. Notice what becomes clearer.

Clarity doesn't require perfection. It requires honesty.

PathFinder Reflection

Picture yourself ten years from now, looking back.

Would you respect the choices you're making today? Would you see alignment—or momentum without meaning?

Authenticity isn't about flawless decisions. It's about aligned ones.

When identity, purpose, and values are clear, work stops feeling like something you endure and starts feeling like something you choose.

And with that clarity in place, the next question becomes unavoidable:

How do you build confidence that lasts—one that is not borrowed from titles, but earned through competence?

CHAPTER 9: LEARNING LOOPS & SKILL STACKING

Careers compound when curiosity compounds

Progress accelerates when learning becomes a system, not an event

Growth is often layered and not just a linear track. The most adaptable professionals don't rely on a single skill, a single role, or a single lane. They build learning loops that repeat, expand, and compound over time. They evolve not by accident, but by design.

Careers don't advance simply because years pass. They advance because insight accumulates—and with it, your usefulness to others.

This chapter explores how PathFinders turn experience into leverage—by closing learning loops, stacking adjacent skills, and pacing growth across seasons so capability compounds instead of stalling.

Why Growth Is Not Linear

Most careers are imagined as ladders: step up, step up, step up. But real growth looks nothing like that. It resembles the rings of a tree trunk—cycles layered over time, each season adding depth and resilience.

Time alone does not create capability. Learning does.

Linear thinking assumes that experience equals progress. PathFinders know better. They build feedback loops around curiosity—small experiments that reveal strengths, surface gaps, and refine direction. Growth comes through iteration, not inertia.

You don't grow because you've been busy. You grow because you've been intentional about what you absorb from the work.

From Depth to Skill Stacking

When I started my career, I saw myself through a single lens: an engineer. My focus was analytical and technical thinking—systems, data, and problem-solving. It was what I went to school for, and I assumed it was what would carry me through the workplace.

But as I looked around at senior professionals and leaders, something stood out. They weren't just technically strong.

They were translators.

They could turn data into insight. They could filter signal from noise and identify the real problem before anyone rushed to solve it. They could explain complex systems clearly. They could connect technical work to business outcomes. And perhaps most importantly, they could tell the story behind the work.

That realization changed how I approached my development.

I made it a personal goal to build those adjacent skills. Whenever an opportunity for training appeared, I raised my hand. When there was a chance to take on work outside my immediate responsibilities, especially if it meant learning something new, I volunteered.

I looked for chances to present to leadership so I could sharpen my communication and storytelling. The work was often uncomfortable at first, but each experience added another layer to the skill set.

Over time, those skills became multipliers.

I wasn't just solving problems anymore. I was aligning people around them. I could translate ambiguous situations into clearer paths forward. Technical depth remained important, but the additional capabilities amplified its impact.

The stacking of those skills shifted my trajectory.

It turned task contribution into influence.

It turned execution into leverage.

Depth gets you started.

Breadth gets you noticed.

Stacking makes you scalable.

The Learning Loop: Do → Reflect → Adjust → Repeat

Most people repeat tasks. Few repeat improvement.

Mastery doesn't come from doing the same thing more times. It comes from tightening the loop between action and reflection.

The PathFinder learning loop is simple:

1. **Do** — Execute the task, project, or challenge.

2. **Reflect** — What worked? What didn't? What surprised you?

3. **Adjust** — What's one shift to test next time?

4. **Repeat** — Integrate the insight before the next iteration.

High performers aren't always the most talented. They're the ones who reflect more deeply and adjust more frequently. They turn every experience into data.

Most professionals collect years. PathFinders collect insight.

Skill Stacking: Portfolios Beat Ladders

Skill stacking is the career equivalent of compound interest. It transforms single-lane specialists into multidimensional contributors.

Some high-leverage stacks include:

- **Analysis + Storytelling** → persuasion with evidence

- **Technical Depth + Empathy** → systems built for real users

- **Creativity + Structure** → innovation that ships

- **Curiosity + Discipline** → learning that converts to execution

Skills don't multiply in isolation. They compound when paired intentionally with adjacent capabilities.

The goal isn't mastery of everything. It's building stacks that multiply value.

Learning as an Operating System

Some days you learn what to do. Most days you learn what not to do. Both count.

Learning isn't a phase of your career—it's the operating system beneath it. The moment learning stops, compounding stops. Curiosity ignites growth. Consistency sustains it.

Growth doesn't require perfection. It requires repetition with awareness.

The 80/20 Rule of Learning

Not all learning lifts equally.

High performers apply focus:

- Invest in the 20% of skills that drive 80% of impact

- Go deep enough to be credible, then broad enough to adapt

- Avoid "perpetual beginner mode"—collecting inputs without integration

Intentional learning compounds. Random learning distracts.

Common Pitfalls

Learning stalls when structure disappears. Watch for these traps:

- **Experience without reflection** — repeating years instead of improving them

- **Skill overload** — collecting tools with no through line

- **Shiny object syndrome** — abandoning depth too early

- **Linear thinking** — believing one promotion defines progress

True growth requires layered clarity rather than scattered ambition.

Productive PathFinder Practice: Build Your Learning Engine

Use this simple rhythm to turn experience into momentum:

1. After your next project, write three lessons learned and one adjustment.

2. Sketch your current skill stack: five core strengths and two adjacent skills to build next.

3. Block one weekly learning sprint—focused, distraction-free.

4. Share one reflection with a mentor or peer to close the loop.

Your learning engine doesn't need size. It needs rhythm.

Pacing Growth Across Seasons

Sustainable careers move in seasons.

There are stretches of intensity—launches, transitions, high stakes. There are also seasons of consolidation and recovery. Balance isn't daily. It's seasonal.

Growth accelerates in spurts. Life adds layers too. Both shape who you become.

Stretching without recovery becomes strain. Recovery without direction becomes drift.

PathFinders name their season, adjust expectations, and pace accordingly.

PathFinder Reflection

Ask yourself:

- What new skill layer have I added this year?

- Where am I repeating patterns instead of refining them?

- What adjacent capability would most multiply my value next?

Growth isn't about aging into experience. It's about evolving into capability.

When learning loops close and skills stack intentionally, confidence stops being borrowed from titles and starts being earned through competence.

And as capability compounds, a new challenge emerges.

Not whether you can do the work, but whether the right people can see it.

ELEVATE

Increase your influence
without losing your center.

CHAPTER 10: STRATEGIC VISIBILITY

Letting your work travel without you

Be so aligned with value that people can't overlook you—even if you're not the loudest in the room.

Great work doesn't always speak for itself. And when it whispers, decision-makers rarely hear it.

Visibility isn't vanity—it's strategy. It ensures your contribution doesn't disappear into busy calendars, shifting priorities, and organizational noise. You're not showcasing yourself. You're clarifying the impact your work makes possible.

Visibility is the bridge between value and opportunity. Without it, even exceptional work fades quietly into the background.

Why Visibility Matters

There's a persistent myth in early and mid-career growth:

If I do great work, people will notice.

Sometimes they do. Often, they don't.

Leaders are often stretched thin. Colleagues are absorbed in their own priorities. Even supportive managers can't advocate for work they never clearly see.

Visibility isn't about drawing attention to yourself. It's about making value legible:

- Here's the problem we solved

- Here's the impact it created

- Here's what others can build on

When framed this way, visibility becomes an act of service. It helps teams learn, strengthens decisions, and prevents progress from disappearing into the blur of execution.

When Work Becomes Visible

During a role transition, I inherited a team whose reputation inside the business unit was surprisingly poor. The external perception was that they struggled to deliver and often slowed progress.

Inside the team, however, the story sounded very different.

They felt overworked and constantly pulled in to fix issues for other functions. Long hours and reactive firefighting were the norm, yet very little of that effort seemed to register beyond the immediate stakeholders.

After spending a few weeks observing the workflow and talking with the team, a different picture emerged.

The internal view was much closer to reality.

The team was doing the majority of the work. What they lacked wasn't execution—it was visibility. There was no narrative around their contribution, no structure capturing the workload, and no consistent way for others to see the impact being delivered.

So, we started by correcting the narrative through data.

First, we built simple data packages that documented the volume and type of work being performed. Execution had always been high, but the work was scattered across emails, hallway conversations, and informal requests. By introducing structure and governance, we created a single repository where work could be tracked and attributed.

Very quickly, the numbers began to tell a different story.

Step one was complete: we could now quantify what had previously been invisible.

Step two was sharing it.

We introduced a weekly report summarizing key activities and progress updates and distributed it to cross-functional leaders. At first, the reports were met with silence. No comments. No replies.

But we kept sending them.

Over time, people began referencing them for updates. Eventually the cadence became the standard reporting format for the business unit.

Suddenly, the work that had always been happening quietly became visible.

Not because the team had started working harder.

But because the work could finally travel beyond the room where it was being done.

The final shift came naturally. Leaders began acknowledging me for the turnaround in performance. While I appreciated the recognition, it was important to redirect the story.

The team had always been performing at a high level.

All we had done was make the work visible.

Within a year, many of those same team members were recognized as high performers and became benchmarks for the rest of the business unit.

Nothing about their effort changed. Only the visibility of their contribution did.

High performers don't always lack impact. Sometimes their work simply hasn't been given a voice.

Visibility Without Ego

Strategic visibility isn't showmanship. It's stewardship.

It shifts attention away from *who did the work* toward *what the work made possible*:

- "This reduced cycle time by two weeks."

- "This clarified a decision that had stalled."

- "Here's a learning the team can reuse."

When visibility is grounded in usefulness, people feel helped—not managed or impressed upon.

Done well, visibility feels like contribution, not performance.

From Visibility to Reputation

Visibility opens doors. Reputation keeps them open.

Over time, people form shorthand narratives:

- "They bring clarity when things get messy."

- "That's who you call when progress matters."

- "They translate complexity into action."

Those narratives shape opportunity—not because you asked for attention, but because your impact became part of the organization's story.

Visibility compounds into trust.

Trust compounds into opportunity.

Practical Ways to Build Strategic Visibility

Visibility isn't a personality trait. It's a system. It isn't about saying more. It's about making value easier to see.

1. Summarize outcomes, not activity

Replace "I worked on…" with "This resulted in…"

2. Share learning, not just progress

Short insights help others and signal thoughtful engagement.

3. Create artifacts

Templates, guides, trackers, and frameworks outlive your presence. Artifacts advocate for your work when you're not in the room.

4. Coach in public

Onboard a new hire. Lead a short session. Teaching is visibility with humility.

5. Connect work to business priorities

Leaders notice what improves flow, reduces risk, or advances strategy.

Common Pitfalls

Strategic visibility avoids both extremes—noise and invisibility.

Watch for these traps:

- **Noise over signal** — speaking often without substance

- **Credit hoarding** — overusing "I" instead of "we"

- **False modesty** — downplaying contributions until they disappear

- **Performative updates** — optics without impact

Say less. Mean more.

Spotlight: Don't Diminish to Fit

Many professionals dim their value to avoid appearing self-promotional.

But minimizing your impact doesn't help others shine. It just keeps your contribution hidden.

You don't need to inflate your work. You need to illuminate it.

Clarity is ensuring alignment over arrogance.

Productive PathFinder Practice: The Impact Log

Maintain a private record of:

- Wins (large and small)

- Problems solved

- Lessons learned

- Positive feedback

- Completed projects

This isn't ego. It's evidence.

Patterns will emerge:

- Where you add distinctive value

- What energizes you

- What others rely on you for

Your log becomes both a mirror and map.

PathFinder Reflection

If someone asked your team today:

"What are they known for?"

What would they say?

Is that the signal you want reinforced?

If not, what clarity does it need—in your actions, your updates, or your focus?

Visibility doesn't begin with recognition. It begins with intention.

When your work travels clearly, opportunity doesn't need to be chased.

It finds you.

CHAPTER 11: DEALING WITH DETOURS

Turning setbacks into direction

Detours are not dead ends. They're data.

Careers rarely unfold the way we imagine them. Roles shift. Teams reorganize. Promotions stall. Leaders change. Sometimes the thing you chased turns out not to be the thing you wanted after all.

The PathFinder mindset doesn't pretend these moments don't hurt. It simply refuses to waste them.

Detours aren't deviations from the path.

They *are* the path.

The Path Is Never Straight

Every meaningful career includes moments that feel like setbacks:

- the role that went to someone else,

- the project that collapsed late,

- the leader who didn't advocate when it mattered,

- the opportunity that disappeared without explanation.

These moments can feel personal—but they're universal.

What separates those who stagnate from those who endure isn't the absence of detours. It's how those detours are interpreted.

PathFinders treat detours as diagnostic in nature.

Not final verdicts.

If something didn't go as planned, it doesn't automatically signal failure. It signals information:

- a gap you didn't know you had,

- a pattern you hadn't noticed,

- a skill the environment quietly rewards,

- a dynamic you underestimated.

Detours don't erase potential. They refine it.

When the Work Doesn't Land

Every project carries a lesson, whether it ends in success or setback.

I once spent over fifteen months working on a strategic initiative with a small core team. Because of the sensitivity around the idea, the work was kept on a need-to-know basis. Only a handful of people were involved.

As the project lead, I facilitated multiple planning sessions, developed several iterations of the business model, and built financial projections showing strong long-term returns. Over time, the direction became clearer. The opportunity looked viable.

Eventually, we reached the point where it was time to bring the proposal to the broader leadership team.

When we presented the idea, however, the reaction was not what we expected.

Instead of enthusiasm, the room was filled with questions, resistance, and hesitation. The discussion quickly shifted from possibility to risk.

In the end, the project was shelved.

After fifteen months of work, the initiative never moved forward.

At first, it stung. A significant amount of time, energy, and thinking had gone into the effort.

But as the frustration faded, the lessons became clearer.

The project itself had been well designed. The financial case was sound. But one critical element had been missing: early stakeholder alignment.

We had built the solution before building the coalition.

The experience reshaped how I approached future strategic initiatives.

From that point forward, I developed a simple template to guide projects of similar scale. The format included an early-stage project charter designed to surface stakeholder perspectives sooner—clarifying expectations, identifying concerns, and aligning on what success would actually look like.

The next time an initiative reached the leadership table, the conversation felt very different.

Detours rarely mean the work was wasted.

More often, they reveal the lesson that makes the next path possible.

Sometimes the value of a project isn't the outcome it delivers.

It's the insight it leaves behind.

The Mindset That Changes Everything

Detours feel painful because they expose how little control we actually have.

One decision can delay your path. One reorganization can reset your scope. One missed moment can shift the timeline you had in your head.

PathFinders internalize a simple truth:

I will succeed. The only question is whether it happens with you—or in spite of you.

This isn't arrogance. It's agency.

Your trajectory isn't defined by a single manager, a single role, or a single year. Momentum finds new outlets. Opportunity reroutes. Growth adapts.

The system may delay you. But it cannot determine you—unless you let it!

Normalize the Pivot

Linear careers are artifacts of a different era.

Modern careers look more like topographical maps—switchbacks, plateaus, unexpected ridges, and sudden drops followed by new climbs.

A missed promotion might redirect you toward work that expands visibility.

A difficult manager might force you to build skills that future-proof your impact.

A closed door might reveal a path you never would have explored otherwise.

Some detours are setbacks. Others are shortcuts disguised as disappointment.

The difference becomes clear only in hindsight—unless you learn to read the terrain while you're still in it.

Failure as Feedback

Detours reveal information you couldn't have accessed otherwise.

After a setback, ask:

- Did I rely too heavily on one sponsor?

- Was my impact visible—or only understood by a few?

- Did I strengthen relationships across the ecosystem?

- Was there a skill gap others could see that I hadn't addressed?

- Was I chasing the role—or the validation that came with it?

The goal isn't to romanticize failure. It's to extract the lesson embedded inside it.

PathFinders don't rush past setbacks. They slow down just long enough to learn—and then move forward with clarity.

Common Pitfalls

Detours only become dead ends when they're misinterpreted.

Watch for these traps:

- **Bitterness** — assuming outcomes are always unfair and shutting down growth

- **Blame** — avoiding accountability and missing the lesson

- **Tunnel Vision** — believing there's only one acceptable path

- **Premature Exit** — leaving before the learning curve has done its work

- **Identity Fusion** — letting one setback define your worth

Detours don't write your story. Your response to them does.

Spotlight: Rebuilding Trust When You Miss

Not all detours are external.

Sometimes you dropped the ball:

- a missed deadline,

- a miscommunication,

- execution that didn't match intent.

Rebuilding credibility is simple—but not easy:

1. Own it clearly. No defensiveness.

2. Communicate the adjustment. Show what changed.

3. Deliver consistently. Let reliability rewrite the narrative.

People don't expect perfection. They respect ownership and growth.

A repaired reputation is often stronger than an untested one.

Productive PathFinder Practice: Your Detour Map

Identify three moments that felt like setbacks.

For each, write:

- What happened?

- What did it reveal about skills, visibility, or relationships?

- What adjustment did it create in your trajectory?

Then identify one open loop:

- an unfinished conversation,

- a relationship left unattended,

- a lesson acknowledged but not applied.

Close it within the next month.

Detours lose power when you turn them into direction.

PathFinder Reflection: Playing the Long Game

Imagine the setback you're facing right now is not an ending—but a redirection.

Ask yourself:

What could make this possible that the original plan could not?

This question doesn't erase frustration. It creates perspective.

Long careers reward resilience.

Enduring careers reward reflection.

Every career includes detours. The question isn't whether they happen—it's how you interpret them.

PathFinders don't fear the bend in the road. They walk into it with curiosity, adjust their stride, and keep moving.

The path is never straight.

But every bend still carries you forward—when you meet it with intention.

AMPLIFY

Let your momentum
lift more than just you.

CHAPTER 12: YOUR CAREER AS A LAB

Prototyping growth without waiting.

The best careers aren't scripted. They're prototyped.

Everyone enters the workforce believing their careers should unfold like a map—clear directions, predictable turns, and guaranteed destinations. But real careers behave more like living systems: adaptive, nonlinear, and shaped by feedback.

The professionals who grow the fastest aren't the ones with the clearest plans.

They're the ones who test, learn, adjust, and iterate.

Career momentum doesn't come from certainty. It comes from curiosity put into motion.

From Planning to Experimentation

Traditional career advice emphasizes planning:

Choose the right path.

Make the right move.

Avoid mistakes.

But planning assumes stability, something modern careers rarely offer. Markets shift. Teams reorganize. Leaders change. Roles evolve faster than job descriptions.

Plans age. Experiments adapt.

PathFinders treat their careers like laboratories. Instead of asking *What should I do next?* they ask:

- What happens if I try this?

- What changes if I approach it differently?

- What can I learn with minimal risk?

In a lab, not every experiment works. But every experiment produces data.

The goal isn't to get it right the first time. It's to learn faster than the environment changes.

When Curiosity Becomes an Experiment

Early in my career, a colleague transitioned out of the business and left a temporary gap in the Operational Excellence (OpEx) team. Rather than simply watching the position sit open, I volunteered to take on the work as a stretch assignment.

There was no promotion attached to it. No change in title. No additional pay.

Just the opportunity to step into a different part of the organization and learn.

For nine months, I immersed myself in the OpEx world. It meant understanding process improvement frameworks, working with teams across functions, and engaging with colleagues from other sites. Through those conversations, we exchanged best practices, compared approaches, and explored different ways of solving the same problems.

What surprised me most wasn't just the new technical tools I picked up.

It was the shift in perspective.

Operational Excellence forced me to look at problems through a systems lens—seeing not just the immediate issue in front of me, but the underlying flow of work, decisions, and dependencies that created it. Many of those ideas began influencing how I approached challenges in my day-to-day role.

By the time the assignment ended, I returned to my original responsibilities with a different toolkit, and a broader view of how the organization actually functioned.

What began as a temporary gap had quietly become an experiment in growth.

That experience reinforced something I've seen repeatedly since.

Careers aren't fixed tracks. They're laboratories.

Some roles teach depth. Others teach perspective. Some assignments confirm your direction. Others reveal paths you didn't know existed.

The goal isn't to predict every step.

It's to stay curious enough to test the next one.

Progress doesn't always come from promotions. Sometimes it comes from experiments.

Why Experiments Work

Career experiments generate two kinds of clarity at once:

- **Value clarity**
  What improves outcomes, flow, or effectiveness around you.

- **Identity clarity**
  What energizes you, stretches you, and reveals where your strengths compound.

This dual return is powerful. As roles evolve and expectations shift, the people who adapt fastest are the ones who have already been testing themselves in small ways.

Instead of waiting for clarity, they create it.

What Career Experiments Actually Look Like

Most experiments aren't dramatic. They're woven quietly into daily work:

- Testing a meeting format that reduces confusion

- Automating a repetitive task

- Reframing metrics to highlight real impact

- Starting a peer learning circle

- Writing a checklist that becomes a shared standard

- Piloting a clearer update to replace bloated status meetings

Each experiment earns two returns:

- Immediate improvement
- Future insight

You learn what works for the system—and what works for you.

Curiosity as a Career Advantage

Curiosity is the through-line across high-growth professionals.

It shows up in:

- the question asked after a missed outcome,

- the process mapped because no one else did,

- the habit tested to reclaim focus,

- the problem solved without being assigned.

Every experiment becomes a learning loop: observe → act → reflect → adjust

Over time, those loops form a personal R&D engine.

Ask yourself:

- What do I solve even when no one asks me to?

- Where do I notice friction others overlook?

- Which experiments energize me enough to repeat?

The answers reveal your operating DNA—the shape of the work you're built to do.

Common Pitfalls

Career labs fail when curiosity loses discipline.

Watch for these traps:

- **Waiting for permission** — assuming experimentation belongs only to leaders

- **Overloading** — running too many tests without reflection

- **Stopping too early** — abandoning experiments before patterns emerge

- **Keeping insights private** — learning without letting the system benefit

Experiments create personal momentum. Shared insights create organizational momentum.

Productive PathFinder Practice: Design Your Lab

Use this loop to build a low-risk growth engine:

1. **Identify three frictions in your current work**

   Where is effort wasted, clarity missing, or flow breaking down?

2. **Turn one friction into a micro-experiment**

   Small enough to run quickly. Big enough to learn from.

3. **Run a two-week test**

   Name your hypothesis: *If I change X, I expect Y.*

4. **Capture what happened**

   What improved? What didn't? What surprised you?

5. **Share one insight**

Momentum compounds when learning travels beyond you.

This loop—observe, test, reflect, share—is how careers evolve without waiting.

PathFinder Reflection: Permission to Tinker

Think about the last month of your work.

Where did you tolerate friction instead of testing a solution?
Where did you stay silent instead of running a small experiment?

What held you back—habit, fear, or uncertainty?

Now ask:

What is one low-risk experiment I can run this week?

Write it down.

Test it.

Learn from it.

Careers aren't managed into greatness.

They're prototyped into it.

Every small experiment adds clarity. Every iteration builds confidence. Every loop sharpens identity.

PathFinders don't wait for certainty. They test for truth.

Your career isn't a script to follow.

It's a lab—alive, adaptive, and rich with data about who you're becoming.

And the most important experiment is always the next one you're willing to try.

CHAPTER 13: PAY IT FORWARD

When momentum becomes legacy

What you build is only half the story. What you share determines the rest.

The final phase of a meaningful career isn't accumulation.

It's contribution.

Not the kind measured in titles or dashboards—but in the number of people who move forward because of something you offered: clarity, encouragement, perspective, or belief.

Success becomes significant when it multiplies.

Why Giving Back Is the Natural Next Step

Momentum shouldn't stop with you. It should start with you.

There comes a point in every Pathfinder's journey when personal growth is no longer the primary constraint. You know how to learn. You know how to adapt. You know how to navigate uncertainty.

What matters next is whether what you've learned stays trapped inside you—or becomes something others can use.

Paying it forward isn't heroism. It's stewardship.

It's the shift from *What can I gain?* to *What can I leave behind that makes the path clearer for someone else?*

You don't need authority to do that. You only need intention.

When Belief Is Borrowed

At one point in my career, a new engineer joined the organization and became a matrixed member of my team.

He had strong technical ability and an exceptional work ethic. It was clear early on that he had potential.

Even though he wasn't my direct report, I started meeting with him regularly. Those conversations gradually expanded beyond immediate tasks into broader discussions about projects, customers, and decision-making. Over time, I began inviting him to sit in on project meetings and customer calls so he could see how those conversations unfolded.

My intention was simple: help him grow into someone who could eventually take on larger responsibilities, perhaps even succeed me one day.

One day, during a customer call, that opportunity arrived sooner than expected.

In the middle of the conversation, I committed the team to delivering a set of outputs within a tight timeline. I knew the work would be challenging, and I also knew he would likely be the one leading much of the effort.

As soon as the call ended, he walked into my office visibly concerned.

We had committed ourselves to something ambitious, and from his perspective it seemed like we had agreed to deliver without fully knowing whether it was achievable.

I asked him to sit down.

Then I told him something simple: I wouldn't have committed to it if I didn't believe he and the team could deliver.

Sometimes the belief arrives before the certainty.

Over the following weeks, he proved that belief was well placed. The team delivered what had been promised, and the experience became a turning point in his confidence.

Over the next year, we built a strong working relationship. He continued to grow, continued to deliver, and continued to take on larger challenges.

Eventually his path led elsewhere. He moved into a different role at another company and never formally succeeded me in the position I'd once imagined.

But that didn't diminish the impact of the experience.

The lessons traveled with him. So did the confidence.

The professional respect remained. And the friendship endured long after the organizational chart changed.

That experience reinforced something I've seen repeatedly in leadership.

Growth compounds when belief is shared.

When someone sees potential in you and creates space for you to stretch, the impact rarely stops with that single moment.

It carries forward into the way you lead others next.

The greatest impact of leadership isn't what you accomplish.

It's what continues through the people you believed in.

Mentorship Is a Posture, not a Position

Many people believe mentorship begins once you reach a certain level.

It doesn't.

Mentorship begins the moment you decide to look back and help someone take their next step.

You mentor every time you:

- share a mistake you once hid

- normalize a question someone is afraid to ask

- explain an unwritten rule

- invite someone into a room they don't yet know how to enter

- celebrate progress others might overlook.

Mentorship isn't about having all the answers. It's about shortening the distance between confusion and confidence.

From Results to Resources

Deliverables solve today's problems. Resources solve tomorrow's.

When you turn your work into templates, guides, playbooks, or lessons learned, you shift from producing outcomes to building infrastructure.

A report closes a loop.

A template multiplies value.

A shared insight becomes culture.

This is the quiet transition from being productive to being generative.

From contributor to force multiplier. From output to impact.

Great careers aren't remembered for what they completed.

They're remembered for what they enabled.

Common Pitfalls

Paying it forward doesn't mean saying yes to everything.

Sustainable contribution requires boundaries.

Watch for these traps:

- **Overextending** — helping so much that your own growth erodes

- **Prescribing instead of sharing** — offering your path as doctrine instead of data

- **Performative giving** — helping for optics instead of impact

- **Stagnating yourself** — forgetting that you're still a learner too

The best givers keep growing. The strongest contributors protect their energy so they can keep showing up.

Because of You, Not In Spite of You

By this point, the question isn't whether you'll succeed.

You already know how to learn. You already know how to adapt. You already know how to navigate complexity.

The deeper question becomes:

Do people succeed because of you—or in spite of you?

Every career leaves a wake.

Some leave confusion, politics, and cleanup. Others leave clarity, confidence, and momentum.

The PathFinder aims to be the second kind.

Influence isn't measured in control. It's measured in contribution.

Productive PathFinder Practice: Pay It Forward Intentionally

Start small. Stay consistent.

- Turn one piece of work into a reusable resource
- Offer to onboard someone new
- Share a lesson you learned the hard way
- Publicly recognize someone doing invisible work
- Create clarity where confusion once lived

You don't need a platform.

You don't need permission.

You just need to begin.

PathFinder Reflection

Think of one person whose path you could make easier.

What do you wish someone had told you earlier?

What did you have to learn the hard way?

What moment of belief would have changed everything for you?

Now offer that gift.

Not someday. Not when you feel "ready." Now.

Because the next generation doesn't need perfect mentors.

They need available ones.

From Momentum to Meaning

The PathFinder Cycle begins with personal momentum. It ends with shared momentum.

Your legacy won't be the titles you held or the goals you achieved.

It will be the people who believed in themselves because you helped them see what was possible.

The seeds you plant today may grow in forests you never walk through.

But their roots will always trace back to you.

And that is how a career becomes a contribution.

CONCLUSION: THE CAREER IS YOURS TO CREATE

You don't climb careers. You build them—piece by piece, season by season, loop by loop.

Ladders promise predictability, but the climb is always dependent on someone else's wall. The PathFinder Cycle offers something sturdier: a flywheel.

Absorb → Apply → Evolve → Elevate → Amplify.

Each turn creates momentum. Each revolution strengthens the one that follows.

That momentum is yours—generated by your systems, clarity, experimentation, and intentional growth. And when the wheel slows down? That's not failure. It's recalibration. You loop back, refine, and push again with more focus than before.

You've built a career engine that no one can take away.

What You've Built Along the Way

Across these chapters, you've constructed far more than a strategy—you've built an inner architecture for long-term growth.

Absorb taught you how to read environments, decode expectations, and treat every moment as data.

Apply turned that learning into progress through small experiments and early action.

Evolve unlocked identity, values, rhythm, and purpose—the core that prevents misalignment.

Elevate taught you influence, visibility, and resilience through detours and complexity.

Amplify expanded your impact—ensuring your growth becomes someone else's foundation.

These were never just chapters. They were stages in your evolution—from contributor to architect, from achiever to multiplier, from success to significance.

The Mindset That Changes Everything

If one idea threads through this book, it is agency.

"I will succeed. The only question is whether it happens with you—or in spite of you."

That sentence reclaims control. It reminds you that timing, titles, and circumstances will shift, but your posture toward growth is constant.

And eventually, the question flips:

"Do others succeed because of me—or in spite of me?"

That is the real test of leadership. Not how far you go, but how many people rise because you rose. Careers end when achievement peaks; legacies begin when contribution multiplies.

The DNA of Work and Life

Work and life aren't opposing forces—they're intertwined strands shaping one another across seasons.

Imagine them like a double helix: sometimes work takes the lead, sometimes life does. They twist, trade tension, and strengthen each other when they move in rhythm rather than competition.

Harmony isn't found in daily balance. It's found in long-term awareness—knowing when to accelerate, when to recover, and when to re-center.

The PathFinder doesn't chase perfection. The PathFinder recognizes seasons and honors them.

The Inner Architecture of Momentum

Every professional eventually faces a choice: become a passenger of your career, or its designer.

Passengers wait for clarity. Designers create it.

They build systems that outlast motivation.

They document lessons so others can benefit.

They approach growth as a craft—iterative, deliberate, and deeply personal.

When you understand that growth itself is a skill, you stop fearing change. You begin engineering it.

The Challenge Forward

This book is not a checklist. It's a compass. And a compass only works if you move.

So, ask yourself:

- What will you **Absorb** tomorrow that you've been overlooking today?

- Where will you **Apply** a new insight this week to sharpen your edge?

- How will you **Evolve** through the next detour instead of shrinking from it?

- Which room will you **Elevate** your voice in next—and why?

- Whose momentum will you **Amplify** before the year is done?

These aren't theoretical prompts.

They are your operating system for progress.

Final Reflection

The career you want won't appear through luck, timing, or someone else's permission. It will emerge from a series of intentional choices, each one compounding on the last.

You already have the tools, the clarity, the confidence, and now, the framework.

You've learned to absorb without imitation, apply without fear, evolve without drift, elevate without ego, and amplify without agenda.

The only remaining question is:

Who will rise because you chose to rise?

And what systems will you leave behind to make their path shorter than yours?

ADDITIONAL RESOURCES

The PathFinder framework is not meant to live on the page. It is meant to live in practice.

These resources are designed to support that translation—from insight to action, from reflection to direction, and from personal growth to expanded perspective. Use them selectively. Return to them often. Let them evolve as you do.

Resource A: The PathFinder Toolkit

Practical tools, exercises, and rituals to turn insight into momentum

The PathFinder Toolkit is a collection of simple, repeatable practices designed to help you operationalize the ideas in this book. These tools align with the five phases of the PathFinder Cycle—**Absorb, Apply, Evolve, Elevate, and Amplify**—and are intentionally lightweight.

They are not checklists to complete once. They are rhythms to return to.

The goal is not perfection. It is momentum that compounds.

Absorb — Learn the Terrain

1. The 10-Minute Debrief

At the end of each workday, jot down:

- What surprised me today?

- What did I learn that I can use tomorrow?

- What friction did I notice?

Ten minutes. Clear perspective.

2. The Alignment Check

Before saying yes to a new task:

- Does this align with my strengths?

- Does it build credibility?

- Does it support where I'm heading?

If two answers are yes, proceed.

If not, pause.

Apply — Turn Insight into Motion

1. Opportunity Map

For two weeks, track:

- Recurring frustrations

- White-space gaps

- Handoff bottlenecks

Circle one and design a micro-experiment to test a fix.

2. The 90-Day Sprint

Choose one short-term focus:

- A skill to sharpen

- A project to stretch

- A system to build

Make progress visible with weekly check-ins.

Evolve — Clarify Identity, Purpose, and Values

1. The Identity Statement

Write 2–3 sentences beginning with: *"I am becoming a person who…"*

This becomes your internal compass.

2. The Values Filter

List your top five values.

Circle your top three non-negotiables.

Evaluate major decisions through them.

3. Purpose Prompt

Complete the sentence:

"I show up each day because…"

Purpose often lives in simple truths.

Elevate — Build Influence and Navigate Detours

1. Visibility Script

When sharing updates:

- Here's the problem we solved
- Here's the impact
- Here's what others can use

Visibility grounded in contribution—not ego.

2. The Detour Debrief

After a setback, ask:

- What did I learn?

- What blind spot did this reveal?

- What pivot does this suggest?

Detours become data when reflected on intentionally.

Amplify — Lift Others as You Rise

1. The Pay-It-Forward Plan (Monthly)

- Highlight one overlooked teammate

- Share one template or tool

- Offer one mentoring conversation

- Convert one deliverable into a reusable resource

Small acts build ecosystems.

2. The Legacy Question

Ask regularly:

"Are people succeeding because of me—or in spite of me?"

PathFinder Rituals

1. Friday Reset (30 minutes)

- Review the week

- Capture lessons

- Set three priorities for next week

Clarity beats chaos.

2. **Sunday Compass (15 minutes)**

   - What matters most this week?

   - Where should I slow down?

   - Where will I stretch intentionally?

3. **Nightly Shutdown (5 minutes)**

   - One win

   - One lesson

   - One focus for tomorrow

Momentum loves consistency.

4. **PathFinder Reminders**

   - Start before you're ready

   - Small steps still count

   - Clarity beats speed

   - Experiments beat expectations

   - No season lasts forever

   - Momentum compounds

   - You don't need permission

   - You are the designer, not the passenger

Resource B: Research Foundations & References

The *Productive PathFinder* framework was shaped by lived experience, reflective practice, and patterns observed across real careers—but it was also informed by decades of research in leadership, learning, organizational behavior, and career development.

The sources below provide the scholarly foundations that reinforce the ideas explored throughout the book, from learning loops and identity formation to mentorship, systems thinking, and contribution at scale.

These works are not presented as prescriptions to follow, but as lenses that have informed the PathFinder Cycle. Readers who wish to explore the academic grounding behind the concepts—without interrupting the narrative flow of the book—will find them collated here for reference, reflection, and deeper study.

Learning, Growth & Adaptability

- Kolb, D. A. (1984). *Experiential learning: Experience as the source of learning and development.* Prentice Hall.
- Eraut, M. (2004). Informal learning in the workplace. *Studies in Continuing Education, 26*(2), 247–273.
- Savickas, M. L. (2013). Career Construction Theory and Practice. In S. D. Brown, & R. W. Lent, *Career Development and Counseling: Putting Theory and Research to Work* (2nd ed., pp. 147-183). John Wiley & Sons.

Leadership, Identity & Influence

- Ibarra, H. (2015). *Act like a leader, think like a leader.* Harvard Business Review Press.
- Northouse, P. G. (2022). *Leadership: Theory and practice* (9th ed.). Sage.
- Kouzes, J. M., & Posner, B. Z. (2017). *The leadership challenge* (6th ed.). Wiley.

Mentorship, Knowledge Sharing & Culture

- Cabrera, Á., & Cabrera, E. F. (2005). Fostering knowledge sharing through people management practices. *The International Journal of Human Resource Management, 16*(5), 720–735.
- Allen, T. D., Eby, L. T., Poteet, M. L., Lentz, E., & Lima, L. (2004). Career benefits associated with mentoring for protégés: A meta-analysis. *Journal of Applied Psychology, 89*(1), 127–136.
- Wang, S., & Noe, R. A. (2010). Knowledge sharing: A review and directions for future research. *Human Resource Management Review, 20*(2), 115–131.

Systems, Organizations & Performance

- Edmondson, A. (2018). *The fearless organization.* Wiley.
- Burke, W. W., & Litwin, G. H. (1992). A causal model of organizational performance and change. *Journal of Management, 18*(3), 523–545.

- Kehoe, R. R., & Wright, P. M. (2013). The impact of high-performance human resource practices on employees' attitudes and behaviors. *Journal of Management, 39*(2), 366–391.

How to Use These Resources

You don't need to read these works to apply the PathFinder Cycle. They are here for readers who want to understand *why* these ideas work, not just *how* to use them.

Return to them when:

- you want language to explain your thinking more clearly,

- you're designing learning or leadership systems,

- or you're mentoring others who want deeper grounding.

Frameworks evolve as curiosity compounds. This resource list exists to support both.

Resource C: Suggested Reading by PathFinder Phase

The PathFinder Cycle was shaped not only by experience and research, but by ideas that challenged assumptions, reframed growth, and expanded how leadership, learning, and careers are understood.

The books below are not required reading. They are lens-shifters, intended to sharpen perspective at different stages of the PathFinder Cycle. Each one aligns to a phase where its ideas tend to land most powerfully.

Use this list as a reference shelf, not a syllabus and return to different books in different seasons.

Absorb — Seeing Clearly Before Acting

These books help you question assumptions, slow down judgment, and read environments more accurately.

- **Think Again** – Adam Grant

  A powerful case for intellectual humility, rethinking, and staying flexible as the world changes. Ideal when you feel certain—but might need curiosity instead.

- **The First 90 Days** – Michael D. Watkins

  A practical guide for decoding new environments and avoiding early missteps during transitions.

- **The Fifth Discipline** – Peter Senge

    A systems-thinking classic that trains you to see patterns beneath events—essential for ecosystem thinking.

Apply — Turning Insight Into Motion

These books emphasize learning through action, execution, and experimentation.

- **Atomic Habits** – James Clear

    A reminder that progress compounds through small, consistent behaviors—not dramatic overhauls.

- **Deep Work** – Cal Newport

    A counterweight to busyness, reinforcing focus, craftsmanship, and meaningful output.

- **Essentialism** – Greg McKeown

    Helps translate clarity into disciplined action by eliminating noise.

Evolve — Identity, Purpose, and Growth Over Time

These books support reflection, alignment, and redefining success as you mature.

- **Designing Your Life** – Bill Burnett & Dave Evans

    A practical application of design thinking to career and life decisions—perfect for experimentation without paralysis.

143

- **Man's Search for Meaning** – Viktor E. Frankl

  A timeless reflection on purpose, resilience, and meaning—especially relevant during detours or misalignment.

- **Range** – David Epstein

  A reframing of non-linear growth and the long game of capability development.

Elevate — Influence, Trust, and Leadership Without Authority

These books focus on credibility, visibility, and shaping outcomes through people—not position.

- **The Five Dysfunctions of a Team** – Patrick Lencioni

  A simple but enduring framework for understanding trust, conflict, and team health.

- **Act Like a Leader, Think Like a Leader** – Herminia Ibarra

  Essential reading for anyone stepping into influence before feeling "ready."

- **The Speed of Trust** – Stephen M. R. Covey

  Reinforces why trust is not soft—it's operational leverage.

Amplify — Contribution, Mentorship, and Legacy

These books explore how impact multiplies when success shifts from personal to collective.

- **Give and Take** – Adam Grant

  A research-backed argument for why generous, thoughtful contributors outperform over time.

- **Multipliers** – Liz Wiseman

  A clear distinction between leaders who drain capability and those who expand it.

- **Leaders Eat Last** – Simon Sinek

  A reflection on leadership as responsibility and service.

How to Use These Resources

Read for resonance, not completion. If a title feels irrelevant today, it may be essential later.

The PathFinder Cycle repeats as does meaning and intent.

Books don't change careers. Application does.

But the right book, at the right moment—can change how you see the path.

AUTHOR'S NOTE

When I started my career, I believed success was about checking the right boxes, the right degree, the right title, the perfectly polished résumé. I thought hard work alone would make the path unfold neatly.

But careers twist. They stall. They redirect. They reveal parts of you that ambition alone can't reach or overcome.

Over time, I learned that success isn't a ladder. It's a structure you build—through systems, relationships, learning loops, and intentional choices that compound.

This book is my attempt to offer what I wish I had then: a practical way to navigate with intention. A framework for transforming experience into clarity. A mindset that treats your career as an evolving craft—one defined not by titles, but by impact.

If you've read this far, thank you. I hope something within these pages sparked a shift in you—a new question, a new courage, a new sense of possibility.

Because the truth is simple:

Your career is not a copy of anyone else's story. It is yours to write, to revise, and to elevate.

Stay curious. Keep moving. Build momentum.

And when the noise gets loud, remember: You will succeed. The only question is whether others succeed *with you—or because of you.*

— **Nigel Pinto**

ABOUT THE AUTHOR

Nigel Pinto is a MedTech engineering leader, systems thinker, and people-focused mentor with over a decade of global experience spanning product development, operations, and advanced manufacturing. He has led high-impact teams across R&D and commercial environments, building scalable systems, strengthening talent pipelines, and guiding complex programs from concept to commercialization.

Known for translating complexity into clarity, Nigel's leadership philosophy blends engineering discipline with human-centered development. His work helps individuals and teams accelerate growth through intentional systems, structured thinking, and practical execution. His guiding principles and frameworks—including the PathFinder Cycle—have supported students, early-career professionals, and experienced leaders navigating change.

Beyond his leadership work, Nigel serves as a board member and community advocate, investing in youth empowerment and workforce development. He is recognized for building high-performance cultures, championing inclusive leadership, and mentoring the next generation of leaders.

Nigel holds advanced degrees in mechanical engineering, is a Lean Six Sigma Black Belt, and is a certified Project Management Professional (PMP®). He is completing his Doctor of Business Administration, where his research focuses on leadership agility and scaling innovation in high-growth environments.

When he's not building systems, teams, or writing, he's exploring the outdoors with his family, experimenting with new ways to think about growth, or quietly developing the next iteration of what it means to be a PathFinder.

Learn more at **productivepathfinder.com**

ACKNOWLEDGMENTS

No one becomes a PathFinder alone. While this book carries my name, it was shaped by the people who influenced my path long before I had the language or courage to describe it.

First, I give thanks to God—for His grace, His providence, and the quiet ways He continues to guide the path.

To my wife—your steadiness, belief, and sacrificial love have built the foundation upon which every chapter of my life rests. You saw who I could become long before I did. Thank you for being my constant, my compass, and the quiet strength behind every milestone.

To my daughter—you transformed ambition into purpose. Every late night, every draft, and every idea in this book was shaped by the hope of becoming someone worth imitating. You will always be my "why."

To the mentors, leaders, and friends who have guided me—thank you for the wisdom, the hard truths, and the unexpected nudges that changed my trajectory. Some of you taught through encouragement, others through contrast. Both have been invaluable.

To the colleagues and teams I've had the privilege of working with—thank you for the trust, the challenges, and the shared pursuit of meaningful work. You reminded me that leadership is not a title, but a responsibility.

To my parents, sister, and extended family—your sacrifices created the runway from which I launched. You instilled in me integrity, resilience, and the value of quiet excellence.

And finally, to the early-career professionals and students I've had the opportunity to mentor—your curiosity and determination have helped shape the PathFinder framework more than you know. This book exists because you reminded me how powerful belief can be when it is shared.

Thank you for walking this path with me. My hope is that these pages make your steps lighter and your journey richer.

— **Nigel Pinto**